BENEATH A ZIMBABWE SUN

BENEATH A ZIMBABWE SUN

GRAHAM PUBLISHING

Published by
The Graham Publishing Company (Pvt) Ltd
P.O. Box 2931, Harare, Zimbabwe

First published 1987
Reprinted 1990, Revised 1996
Reprinted 1998, 2000, Revised 2002, 2005 & 2007

Publisher and Editor: Gordon M. Graham
Compiler: Eric Edwoods
Text Author: Beverley Whyte
Wildlife Consultant: Gavin Ford
Photographic Consultants: David Trickett, Hans Uhlarz
Art Director: Michael Austin

Origination by Hans Uhlarz
Printed and bound by Tien Wah Press (Pte) Ltd,
Singapore

ISBN 0 86921 039 4

CONTENTS

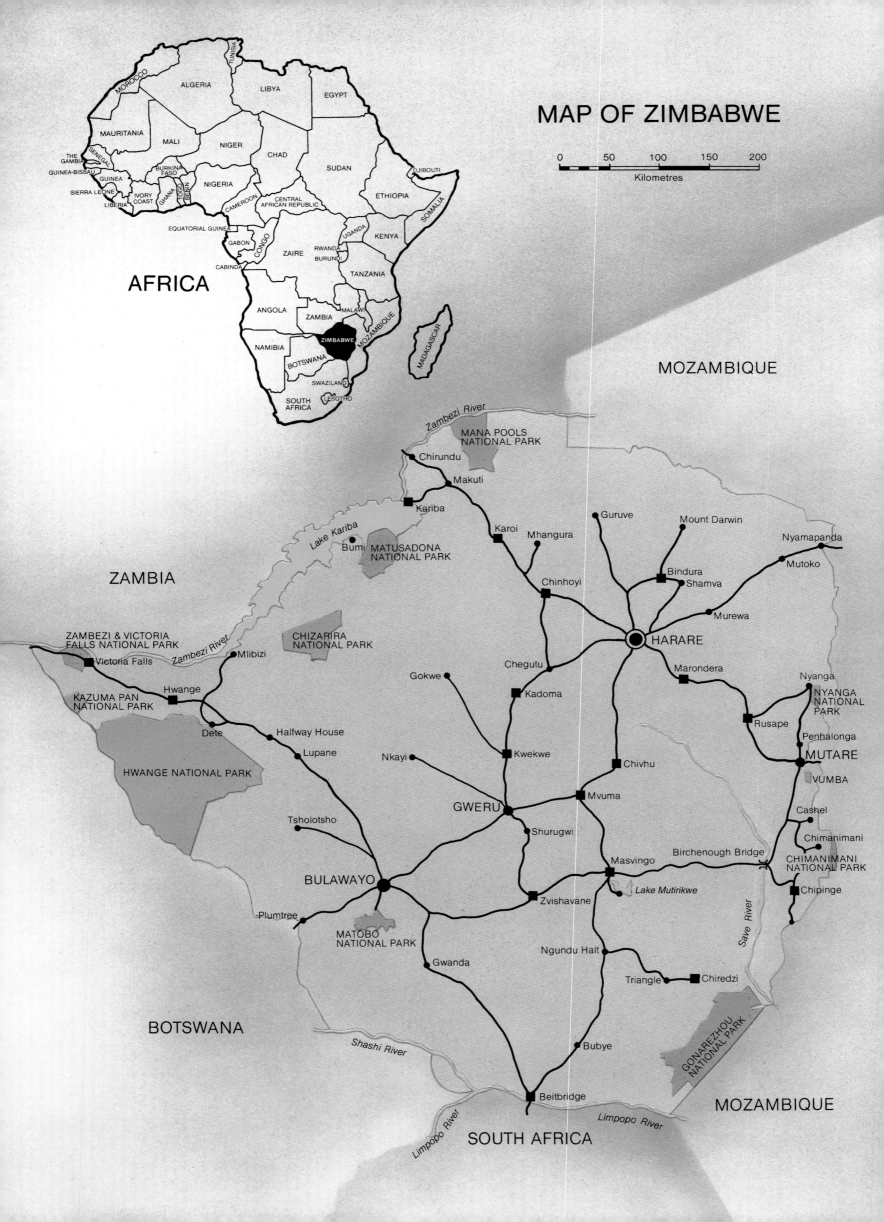

MAP OF ZIMBABWE

AFRICA

Scale: 0 50 100 150 200 Kilometres

ZIMBABWE
An Eden of Contrasts

ZIMBABWE is a song which, once heard, is never forgotten; a mood to suit the needs of any soul, any time; a spell that binds all those who know her.

Her voice brings forth many melodies: the exultant shriek of a Fish Eagle high above the opalescent vastness of a dawn on Kariba; the sibilant hush of silver gums in a noon-day Nyanga forest; the poignant notes of a marimba as sunset bleeds the sky over a village.

Her moods are as varied and captivating as those in any feminine personality. She can be as serene as a verdant Bromley valley; as exotic as the Vumba, where orchids and monkeys tangle in the lianas; as wild and untrammelled as the lion-coloured plains of Hwange; as lonely and mystical as Chimanimani, a place of silence and stillness, broken only by the scimitar flight of an eagle arcing in and out of the high grey clouds.

4

Her cities too, have widely divergent faces. Harare is Zimbabwe dressed up to go out— sophisticated, glittering, elegant, with a febrile pulse. Bulawayo has a warm, maternal air, disdaining too many formal trappings, its capacious streets beckoning like open arms. Mutare has a fresh, demure charm that entrances all who see her—"there is neither sea nor snow, but there is everything else!" wrote Evelyn Waugh. Gweru is friendly and tomboyish, adapting to a busy adult life as the head of the bustling industrial Midlands, but still retaining a kick-off-your-shoes air.

How to analyse Zimbabwe's magic? It is an ancient and heady brew. The Zambezi Valley cradled *Brachiosaurus* (the largest animal to walk the earth) and, very specially, its very own *Syntarsus rhodesiensis*, a small feathered creature that existed nowhere else in those infant years on earth.

Sapphire Kariba in all its immensity covers the happy hunting ground of yet another unique dinosaur, *Vulcanodon karibaensis*, which bridged the gap between the dinosaurs and subsequent giants such as the sauropods. Here, and in the adjacent Zambezi Valley, was where evolution stirred and quickened in the world's womb. Its most notable baby was man. Theory has it that, in the south-central part of Africa, he first hauled himself to his feet. In the beginning, he closely resembled an ape, but it was in these surroundings that he began to think in a non-simian manner, to communicate in words, to invent. He was then what we know now as *Australopithecus africanus*, but he was to evolve into *Homo sapiens*, to multiply throughout Africa and, thereafter, other continents. But perhaps there was indeed a fairy godmother at his christening, for Nature saw to it that for millennia, while Europe and Asia were filling up with

seething humanity, his birthplace remained largely empty of all but flora and fauna.

The first to inhabit Zimbabwe were Bushmen, a small nomadic people who, despite their peripatetic way of life, had a profound artistic instinct and were bent on recording all the beauty around them for posterity. On the walls of their cave homes, they drew thousands of delicate murals, colouring them with dyes from berries, herbs and barks. Many of them remain, as vivid two thousand years later as any wildlife photograph, capturing the arabesque of a leaping inpala, the coquettish caprice of a zebra.

Then came the Bantu migration from Africa's great lakes downwards. As they moved, sections dropped out to settle *en route*, but many reached Zimbabwe. By AD 800 the Tonga and Tavara in the Zambezi Valley and the Karanga, in what is now the Masvingo Province, were settled in. The Karanga built an enormous structure which was named Great Zimbabwe, or Great House of Stone, and it was occupied as a citadel by their king. For centuries, the Karanga and the succeeding Rozvi dynasties ruled supreme, and eventually their kingdom stretched from the Gwayi River to the Indian Ocean. At the zenith of Great Zimbabwe's glory, it received visitors from the outside world, including Arab traders who came in their hordes, bearing trinkets, silk and exotica in exchange for sacks of gold and ivory.

Less welcome were the Portuguese who, in the early 16th century, thought they would colonise Zimbabwe, but their band of soldiers and priests failed; and peace thereafter fell over the land until in the 1880s a man called Cecil Rhodes saw her as the glittering prize in his Cape-to-Cairo master plan. Purporting to seek only mining concessions, and promising King Lobengula rifles, ammunition, money and a gunboat on the Zambezi—none of which ever materialised—he stole a country, and occupied it with an invading force in the name of his Queen, Victoria.

The rest is chronicled in history books, and was etched in blood across the lovely face of Zimbabwe. But in 1980 the guns fell silent and hands stretched out to meet each other as a new nation was born.

The visitor's immediate impression of Zimbabwe is of genuine goodwill, the warm friendship that permeates the country from border to border, and of the beauty that is its inheritance. Linger over the pages that follow and, whether the Zimbabwe they conjure up is a new experience or a part of your life, the essence of her, like a love beyond all telling, will return to haunt you. But happily.

HARARE has been described as "The Pearl of Africa", but the city (previously Salisbury) is more like a diamond—sparkling, glamorous, many-faceted. Yet it wasn't always so. Chief Harare, who ruled the area before Cecil Rhodes' invasion, had wisely chosen to site his headquarters further south than the muddy clearing where the British column hauled up its Union Jack in September 1890. The first Fort Salisbury was a marshy place and its early years of growth into a town were hampered by the fact that, when the rains came and the rivers flooded, no supplies of any sort could reach it, sometimes for weeks on end. White women were banned for the first two years by order of the misogynistic Rhodes, but Vicomte de la Panouse circumvented that when he smuggled in his beloved Fanny Pearson, disguised as his manservant "Billie". Soon the town was home to a motley assortment of remittance men (the self-styled Bishop of Hong Kong staged the most successful cons); eccentrics (the Irish Giant, 1,5 m tall, would fight anyone for a drink) and *poules de luxe* (Diamond Lil had a sparkler embedded in her front tooth). In stark contrast were the folk heroes of that time—most prominently, Ambuya Nehanda and Kaguvi—who ral-

lied their own people to rise up for the First Chimurenga (War of Liberation) and were hanged in 1897. They were spirit mediums, and are believed to speak through successors today. Their names and likenesses can be found on buildings, plaques and sculptures in modern Zimbabwe.

The railway came to Salisbury in May 1899. In 1913, Cleveland Dam made a piped water supply possible, and Seke Dam followed. After the First World War, tobacco boomed as a crop, and newfound "barons" hired permanent suites in Meikles Hotel. By 1935, light industries and factories were springing up.

Since Independence, on April 18th, 1980, the city that is now Harare has burgeoned. It boasts shopping malls, cinemas, theatres, night clubs, horseracing—and more cultural pleasures. The National Archives has a priceless collection of maps, sketches, books, diaries and documents, as well as most of Thomas Baines' paintings. The National Gallery holds frequent exhibitions of both indigenous and foreign works of art. The National Museum's speciality is the Story of Man and the Story of Animals in Mashonaland—and also has the largest collection of birds' eggs in Africa, with over 16 000 specimens.

Ten minutes from the city you'll find Chapungu Kraal, in pastoral surroundings, where there is a magnificent collection of soapstone and verdite sculpture (verdite being the emerald green stone unique to this part of Africa) and an authentic 19th century Shona village complete with *n'anga* (witchdoctor).

Epworth's Balancing Rocks, 11,2 km from Harare, are primeval architecture at its most weird and spectacular; and for a different mood, take the Golden Stairs Road to the Mazowe Valley, half an hour's drive away. Here the 21 853 ha citrus estates stretch across a green valley backed by hyacinth-coloured mountains. The valley is irrigated by the 445 ha Mazowe Dam which is a delight for yachtsmen and anglers—the second-largest carp ever caught on rod and line was landed here in 1965.

Mazowe's bigger sister, Lake Chivero, lies to the west of the city. Watersports of all kinds are available on the resort-filled north shore, but the south shore is 2 023,4 ha of fascinating wilderness, where zebra, giraffe, sable, white rhino, tsessebe and eland roam. Bird life is so prolific that, in one day, ornithologists recorded 200 species. In the granite hills you can find many Bushmen paintings. Lodges and chalets on the lake shore are available.

Near the lake, Viv Bristow's Lion Park is a special pleasure. Half is given over to natural bushveld, where many lions lounge on rocks, sprawl in the shade of huge indigenous trees, or wrestle with their cubs in the sunlight. In the fenced section, the animals range from leopard to otter. A few minutes' drive away, Larvon Bird Gardens with their breathtaking array of indigenous and exotic birds, and the Snake Park, are added attractions.

Drive out of Harare to Kadoma which began in 1906 as a forwarding agency to serve the needs of gold mines in the vicinity. Now it is the centre of Zimbabwe's textile industry. Kadoma is in the midst of a prolific agricultural region—cotton, beef cattle and maize are its most renowned products, but tobacco and dairy do well here too.

Kwekwe gained its name from the croaking of frogs in the nearby river. In fact, four rivers meet here—the Umniati, Sebakwe, Kwekwe and Gweru—and irrigate a cornucopia of farmlands famed for their maize and winter wheat. The sandveld region east of the town is ideal for cattle. Few ranches are under 8 000 ha. Kwekwe was originally a gold mining camp and is today characterised by the large mines in its vicinity producing gold, chrome and iron. ZISCO, with its satellite town of Redcliff, is the centre of Zimbabwe's steel industry.

There are two attractive dams in this region: Sebakwe and Ngezi. Sebakwe, set in a 8 093 ha national park, has a spectacular cliff setting, and abundant bird life. Sable, kudu, wildebeest and zebra come down to the water's edge to drink at sunset. There is sailing and boating, and bream, bottlenose and vundu for the angler. Ngezi, a 360 ha dam in a 580 ha national park, has beguiling coves and inlets, and a backdrop of the grape-shadowed Mashava Hills to the west. Yellowfish and barbel are to be found in its waters, and there is also much game to be seen. Cottages and camping sites are available at both dams.

Gweru, capital of the Midlands Province, gained a reputation as the thirstiest town in the country. Established in 1894 when gold fever had struck, within six months it boasted six hotels. Few of the prospectors ever made their fortunes, but now there are some sizeable gold mines in the area, as well as those producing chrome, asbestos, iron, coal, limestone and tungsten. Gweru was also famous for its post pole—passing carriages and wagons would halt to check here for mail. In 1902 the railway arrived and boosted growth. Today there are factories producing an enormous variety of goods; and grain milling and dairy products reflect the rich farmland surrounding the city. Close by lies Gwenoro Dam, excellent for sailing, boating, water skiing and bream fishing.

Matabeleland has a long turbulent history. 150 000

5

years ago, Stone Age man roamed its wooded valleys and great rocky outcrops. As Europe emerged from the Dark Ages, a sophisticated black race was building intricate stone structures on the banks of the Kame River, and establishing a cattle and grain crop industry.

Then in the early 19th century, Mzilikazi, a Zulu chief in South Africa, quarrelled with the mighty chief Chaka and, with his supporters, fled north. His final settling place was a plain beneath a hill which he pointed out as a landmark to his *indunas* (military chiefs), which has since been known as Ntabazinduna, and he was proclaimed King.

Mzilikazi died in 1868 and, after some years of internecine strife, his son Lobengula succeeded him. Bitterly, Lobengula said: "I have been 'killed' by my people. I will call my kraal Gubuluwayo (meaning he who has been hunted down and killed)." Here he ruled until his *impis* (regiments) were defeated by Rhodes' invading forces in 1893. From the smoking ruins of the royal kraal, the new Bulawayo was to rise.

Rhodes insisted that the streets of the new town were to be laid out in the grid pattern of an imperial Roman settlement, and that each should be wide enough to allow a wagon and a full span of 16 oxen to make a complete turn. The result is a city of light and space, with a welcoming *ambiance*.

6

The arrival of the railway in 1897 laid the foundation for Bulawayo's fortunes, and since then it has been the headquarters of the National Railways of Zimbabwe. Bulawayo is also the hub of Matabeleland's vast ranching industry, but it has a large industrial complex. The region contains many mines too—with abundant deposits of asbestos, chrome, copper, gold, mica, nickel, tin and semi-precious stones, including the famed grass-green Sandawana emeralds.

The city has many attractions for the visitor: the Railway Museum, with its antique rolling stock; the Colosseum-style Natural History Museum which houses a 75 000-specimen mammal collection; the surrounding Centenary and Central Parks including an aviary, a miniature steam railway and a multi-hued fountain; the Mzilikazi Arts and Crafts Centre, as well as modern shops, cinemas and nightclubs.

Bulawayo is ringed by a blue necklace of dams: Hillside, only six kilometres south, has a nature reserve, an aviary and a picnic site; a little further are Ncema, Umzingwane and Kame. For those who like to see wildlife at closer quarters, the Chipangali Wild Life Orphanage has an enchanting collection of orphaned and once-injured animals and birds.

Thirty kilometres outside Bulawayo lies the most spectacular treat of all: the Matobo National Park. In prosaic terms, it comprises 2 000 sq km of granite outcrops, estimated to be 3 000 million years old, 70 sq km of which make up the national park. Mzilikazi named it, referring to the great round rocks as *matobo* or "the bald-headed ones". Here Nature has created an unparalleled sculptural display, ranging from a cosy giants' tea party tumble of brown buns to an Easter Island monolith rubbing shoulders with what must surely be the head of a dinosaur—but a little further on, the sun illuminates a bronze Camelot look-alike of crenellations, ramparts and turrets. Within the nation-

al park, white rhino, giraffe, eland, zebra and sable are to be found. Tranquil Maleme Dam, where there are cottages and camping sites, is a favourite haunt for water birds.

The ancients sought to embellish this natural gallery in their own exquisite way. Many caves contain Bushmen paintings—feast your eyes on the giraffe, elephant and kudu depicted in Nswatugi cave; the tsessebe, elephant, steenbok, mongoose, giraffe, warthog and human hunters of Bambata cave; Silozwane's frieze, and Gulubahwe's 4,5 metre long undulating snake, carrying on its back humans, baboons and buck.

"Nothing has changed since the time of the gods, neither the running of water nor the ways of love", says a Japanese poem. Move from the Bushmen murals to a national park pool where a pair of giraffe shyly nuzzle each other and you perceive the truth of the words.

Bulawayo is the best starting point for a move to the region many feel is the most dramatic in Zimbabwe—Hwange and Victoria Falls. The road leads through Matabeleland at its most unspoilt—a harsh, rugged bush landscape, characterised by a tangle of thorn scrub here, a sudden forest of great indigenous trees there, interspersed with the limitless grassy plains.

At the turn of the century, the Hwange region was known as "the white man's grave"—a place of blazing heat, whose denizens were ferocious lion, all too ready to attack invaders. One man had the yoke on his oxen bitten in two when a lion leapt at the team.

In 1893, a German prospector, Albert Giese, heard reports from local villagers of "stones that burnt" which they used as fuel for their fires. He decided to investigate and journeyed north as far as Victoria Falls—but when he learnt that Matabele warriors were on the march, he beat a hasty retreat. A year later, he tried again, and this time found deposits of coal. He pegged the first coal-mining location in the country on an outcrop of shale 9,15 metres thick, exposed in the bed of the Kamandana River. In 1895, a concession of 1 036 sq km was pegged and obtained by the Mashonaland Agency. Production of coal began in 1903 and today the collieries are amongst the world's richest. Hwange is more than coal, however. The town stands sentinel to Zimbabwe's most spectacular national park. Here some of the largest and most varied concentrations of wild animals to be seen in Africa roam freely.

Hwange is only 112 km south of Victoria Falls, Africa's mightiest waterfall. Geologists set its age at 150 million years. At that time, hot volcanic lava oozed through the earth's crust. When it cooled and contracted, it formed crevices. The flooding Zambezi River caused the crevices to recede, creating cavernous gorges. Five waterfalls developed: the Devil's Cataract, Main Falls, Horseshoe Falls, Rainbow Falls and Eastern Cataract. The lowest is 61 metres, the highest 108 metres. Emerald grass, trees and exotic flora of the Rain Forest, and glistening black basalt rock set the stage for this, Nature's most splendid and enduring drama.

The Victoria Falls are one of the world's wonders. Their mother country is a fitting backdrop indeed.

1 (dustjacket), **2** (title page) and **3** (contents page)
Zimbabwe's magnificent sunsets are the most lasting, and photographed, memories visitors take home with them. Whether it is elephant or Fish Eagle silhouetted against a blaze of golds and yellows at Kariba or a fiery orb lowering majestically behind a mountain in the Eastern Highlands bathing the valleys below in its warmth, it is imagery that is long remembered—and cherished.

4 The mystical ruins of Great Zimbabwe appear to symbolise the rising of the new nation like a phoenix from the ashes of history. (See page 74.)

5 The mighty Victoria Falls, one of the greatest wonders of the world, is Zimbabwe's most internationally-known attraction. (See page 96.)

6 The Chimanimani Mountains have always seemed to hold lofty court over the impossibly lush and fertile Eastern Highlands and to present an irresistible challenge to climbers. (See page 56.)

7 Jacaranda time in Harare. The trees were imported from South America in the shape of a few tiny seedlings at the turn of the century and now cloak the entire city in a purple mist come October. Here in the city's Africa Unity Square, they provide a welcome carpet to Meikles Hotel which, in a survey conducted by a British travel magazine, was voted the tenth best hotel in the world and the best in Africa.

8 The aesthetic lines of Livingstone House, erected in the 1950s and the first multi-storey building the city could boast, soars as a backdrop to the serenity of Harare Gardens.

9 Harare, Zimbabwe's capital, contrasts vividly between skyscrapers and green pockets which are a feature of the city. At 1 500 metres above sea level and with an annual rainfall of 760 mm, it enjoys one of the most healthy and delightful climates in the world.

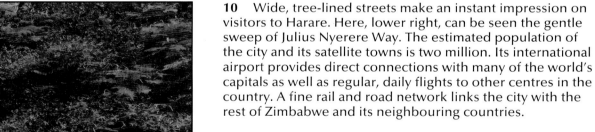

10　Wide, tree-lined streets make an instant impression on visitors to Harare. Here, lower right, can be seen the gentle sweep of Julius Nyerere Way. The estimated population of the city and its satellite towns is two million. Its international airport provides direct connections with many of the world's capitals as well as regular, daily flights to other centres in the country. A fine rail and road network links the city with the rest of Zimbabwe and its neighbouring countries.

11　First Street Mall, the heart of Harare city. Originally a busy tangle of traffic-laden streets, it has been closed off to form a peaceful shopping mall, frothing the year round with greenery.

12　Harare's beautiful Botanical Gardens are adorned with a myriad species of indigenous trees and shrubs as well as exotica. Here, its superb winter aloe and cacti collection is in flower.

13　A Saturday afternoon turf battle nears its climax. Racing at Borrowdale is a social as well as a sporting feature of the Harare week.

14　In November and December, the blooms of the flamboyant trees follow those of the jacarandas to create an appropriately red and gold Christmastime spectacular throughout the city and its suburbs, as here in a quiet avenue.

16

19

17

18

15 A march-past by members of the Zimbabwe National Army during Independence Day celebrations at Rufaro Stadium, Harare, commemorating the country's attainment of nationhood on April 18th, 1980.

16 The Opening of Parliament. Crowds are attracted by the pomp and ceremony of the arrival of the President, escorted by mounted police, to open Parliament.

17 At each new sitting of Parliament, the prelude to the official opening is an inspection of the armed guard by the President. Then a 21-gun salute booms out over Africa Unity Square, scattering the pigeons into the air and evoking ululations from the crowd.

18 VIP visitors are always given a rousing welcome in the traditional manner at Harare International Airport.

19 Heroes' Acre is a 15-minute drive from the Harare city centre. Here, leading figures who perished during the War of Liberation are buried and commemorated. The memorial's pinnacle, seen here, symbolises the men and women who fought side by side.

20

22

21

20 Zimbabwean pottery and soapstone carvings are objects of beauty and imagination. Animal life or facial studies, they are often artistically powerful, always acceptable, and are found amongst the wares of the roadside artists themselves and in the shops.

21 The annual Harare Show is a week-long event crammed with agricultural, industrial and home crafts displays and a host of entertainments from sky-diving to police dog displays and prancing drum-majorettes.

23

22 The Flame Lily *(Gloriosa superba)*, Zimbabwe's national flower, is a specially protected plant.

23 Cricket at Harare Sports Club. Sport is not so much a hobby as an intrinsic part of life in Zimbabwe. Almost every type of sport, apart from skiing, has a following—from rugby to baseball, hockey to karate. Every weekend without fail the nation's stadiums are packed for a football match.

24 Rising tall and slender above Harare Gardens is the Holiday Inn Crowne Plaza Monomatapa, one of many hotels catering for the needs of Zimbabwe's tourists.

25 Warm and secure, this is the traditional way for babies to travel in Africa.

26 The Rainbow Towers Hotel and Conference Centre, right. Seating up to 4 500 delegates, the Centre's auditorium can be separated into independent committee rooms, enabling different events to be held simultaneously. Each seat contains a folding table and sound controls for instant translations.

27

18

28

29

27 Lake Chivero, 32 km from Harare, is the city's main water supply. Formed by the building of the Manyame Poort Dam on the Manyame River in 1952, Chivero is part of a national park and game reserve. Here, either from comfortable chalets or on day trips, visitors and residents can see a variety of wildlife in natural habitat—square-lipped (white) rhino, zebra, tsessebe, impala, wildebeest.

28 Lake Chivero is more than a water source for Harare residents: resorts, fishing and boating clubs and picnic sites are very popular, and at weekends the waters are busy with yachts, speedboats and aquaplanes, as here at the Jacana Yacht Club.

29 The graceful African Jacana— known colloquially as the Lily Trotter because of its habit of using lily pads as stepping stones—is a familar sight at Lake Chivero.

30 Near Lake Chivero is the Lion Park. Privately run, half of it is given over to natural bushveld where dozens of lion lounge on rocks, sprawl in the shade of huge indigenous trees or wrestle with their cubs. In the other, fenced, section there is a comprehensive collection of animals ranging from leopard to otter.

31 A chameleon, this fearsome-looking creature is only 15 cm long and eats grasshoppers, butterflies and insects which he catches with a tongue as long as his body. What appears to be a perfect set of teeth are labial scales and he really is quite harmless—Zimbabwean children often keep chameleons as pets.

32 Built on the leeward side of a stony ridge scattered with baobab trees, this rural family village blends well with the harsh, dry scrub. The building of such a village is a co-operative effort and neighbouring families work with a will, knowing that *nhimbe* or *utshwala* (beer) has been brewed and celebrations will follow. The cutting and setting of the poles is the task of the men. The women are responsible for plastering the walls with *daga* (mud) and the floors with a mixture of mud and cow dung, which will subsequently take a high polish. Only men work on the roof, lashing poles together and applying the thatch.

33 There are faces which are the landscape of Africa in themselves, hewn from rock, weathered by wind and rain. Wisdom, born of experience, is etched in this old man's face. Greying hair is respected and custom decrees that all who come to village elders for advice show due respect.

34 Young boys (and girls) in the rural areas have the responsibility of keeping watch over the family cattle, sheep and goats. This task is not to be taken lightly as, more often than not, the wealth of the family lies in its livestock. The very young children will watch over the sheep and goats, enjoying a relatively carefree life, until they are old enough to enter formal school. When they are older, they will be responsible for the cattle.

32

33

34

35

35 The Wood Ibis is a familiar sight on river banks. This is part of a breeding colony in the upper reaches of the Zambezi River and the parent, here, is standing over its chick in the thick riverine vegetation.

36 Ewanrigg Gardens, 40 km from Harare on the Shamva Road, contain the most comprehensive collection of aloes, cycads and cacti in Zimbabwe. The gardens are at their best from June to August when these spectacular plants are in their pink and yellow glory. There are other attractions, too, as well as picnic facilities for those who want to make a day of it.

37 The cathedral-size Chinhoyi Caves with their Sleeping Pool lie eight km from Chinhoyi on the Kariba Road. The caves descend 50 metres to the pool which is overhung by giant stalactites wreathed in creepers. Free from organisms and sediment, its limpid depth of 85 metres is lit at midday by a shaft of sunlight making the water appear impossibly blue. The pool is best viewed from the Dark Cave, known as the Coal Hole. The traditional name for the Sleeping Pool is *Chirorodziva*, "Pool of the Fallen", because, when Chief Chinhoyi took refuge in the caves in 1830 (the customary sanctuary of his people), invading warriors found a way in and hurled many of his followers to their death in the pool. Today, though, no ghosts linger in this beautiful place.

38 Kopjes are found within a 15-minute drive of most cities and towns. These huge stone hills are formed by the natural stripping of layers of granite. Some are also the result of weathering of enormous granite rocks causing them to break up into large irregular blocks, sometimes balanced precariously one on top of another.

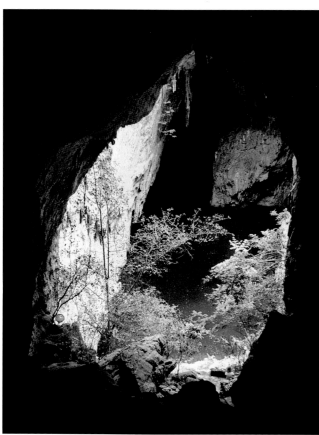

36

37

38

39

40

39 & 40 Sculptures . . . fashioned by nature, as seen in the balancing granite rocks at Epworth, outside Harare; and by man, as manifested in this soapstone head. Zimbabwean sculpture, much of which is rooted in mythology, is justly renowned throughout the world, but nature's own creations are as powerful and evocative.

44

45

43

41 Zimbabwe contains some of the most exquisite examples of Stone Age art in the shape of its Bushmen paintings, as here in a series of caves near Bindura. Tiny, nomadic hunters, the Bushmen decorated the walls of their cave homes with recordings of the wealth of animal life which surrounded them (elephant, rhino, kudu, etc.) and of their exploits in the field. Berries and lichens formed the dyes which have lasted for well over a thousand years.

42 This rock face, at the Bindura site, with its honeycomb of caves was a typical Bushman haunt. The natural surroundings provided excellent camouflage and, when threatened by marauding outsiders, the Bushmen could take shelter inside their stony fortresses. The entrance to this cave can just be seen behind the small trees and bushes in the centre of the picture.

43 Weathering and the seepage of water over the centuries have combined to create remarkably beautiful surrealistic friezes on the rock face.

44 The Malachite Kingfisher is one of nine varieties of kingfisher to be found in Zimbabwe. A spectacularly-coloured bird, it eats fish which it catches by diving from a low perch into the water. Judging by its wet breast feathers, this kingfisher has just returned from such a hunt.

45 The lovely Wild Wisteria (*Bolusanthus speciosus*) is a delight for all who come across it in the bushveld in September and October when its lilac-blue flowers are in bloom. The wood is very hard and excellent for axe handles and fencing posts as it is ant- and borer-proof.

46 One can almost see the edge of time from the awe-inspiring World's View in the Matobo Hills. Its traditional name is *Malindidzimu*, "The holes in which the spirits dwell", since its spiritual familiars are said to guard the tomb of Mzilikazi, the first king of the Matabele, who died and was buried in the Matobo Hills in 1868, 30 km from Bulawayo.

47 A particularly splendid example of balancing rocks stands sentinel at the entrance to the Matobo National Park. A vast natural wonderland, the park extends over 47 400 ha, and includes gentle Maleme Dam and a game park which extends over 6 700 ha.

48 Another vista from World's View is one of unforgettable rough grandeur: a giant playground of granite hills stretching as far as the eye can see.

49 Natural granite domes and castles. Erosion and exfoliation by the elements in even layers, known as onion-skin peeling, brought about the smooth, rounded appearance of the whalebacks.

50 The changelessness of eternity that is peculiarly Matobo deeply affected Cecil Rhodes. When he came across this huge granite outcrop, commanding an unparalleled view of the timeless countryside, he exclaimed, "The peacefulness of it all . . . the chaotic grandeur . . . I call this one of the views of the world", and directed that he should be buried here.

47

48

49

50

51

52

51   The winding road to the Matobo Hills. The kopjes are favourite haunts of the handsome Black Eagle, which is frequently seen soaring above them. The national park has the densest breeding population in the world of this magnificent bird of prey.

52   Rock formations consist of castle kopjes and whalebacks. Kopjes comprise boulders in every shape and size, seemingly arranged together in an almost endless variety of compositions, as here, for example, with the "Mother and Child" balancing rocks in the Matobo Hills. The whalebacks are rocks which resemble bald heads.

53   A Plum-Coloured Starling feeds its young in a natural tree-hole nest in the Matobo National Park where it breeds. This is the male as the female lacks the brilliant colouring, being mottled-brown on the back and off-white streaked on the breast.

54   At Maleme Dam in the Matobo National Park, comfortable lodges (as shown here), cottages and chalets with commanding views are provided. There are also caravan and camping facilities.

55   Backed by the magnificent wooded Matobo Hills, Maleme Dam is one of Zimbabwe's loveliest stretches of water. Bulawayo residents flock here every weekend, and for longer periods, to fish, sail and picnic or simply to enjoy its inimitable beauty and tranquillity.

56

57

30

56 Giraffe are common in the game park in the Matobo National Park where they breed successfully and have been part of the landscape since time immemorial. However, the original giraffe population here was hunted to extinction by the early settlers and the species was translocated from Hwange National Park.

57 Square-lipped (white) rhino at Matobo. "White" is a misnomer, since their colour is virtually indistinguishable from that of the hook-lipped (black) rhino. The "white" arises from an Afrikaans word meaning wide, referring to its large, square lips. As with the giraffe, the white rhino was hunted to extinction here and the present population is descended from the re-introduction of the animals in the 1960s from Natal in South Africa.

58

59

60

58 Cyrene Mission, 32 km from Bulawayo, is run by the Anglican Church and is renowned for producing a wealth of artistic talent. Richly carved furniture and splendid murals are on display here, all created by pupils.

59 As Europe emerged from the Dark Ages, a sophisticated people was building an intricate stone structure on the banks of the Kame River. Thought to be over 300 years old, the Kame Ruins are the second largest after Great Zimbabwe with which they have links in style because of the dry-stone building technique. With a superb view of the wooded country of Kame, the Ruins have a charisma, are 22 km from Bulawayo and are well worth a visit.

60 A baby elephant enjoys a snack at the Chipangali Wildlife Orphanage, 23 km from Bulawayo. Founded by Mr Viv Wilson to provide a home for orphaned and injured or disabled animals and birds, this fascinating complex has become world-known through the popular television series, "Orphans of the Wild".

61 Prosperous, attractive and friendly, with a population of about 800 000, Bulawayo is Zimbabwe's second largest city. One has the feeling of spaciousness in Bulawayo because of its particularly wide thoroughfares: when the streets were laid out in 1894, it was decided that they should be wide enough to allow a wagon and a full span of 16 oxen to make a complete turn. The city has an annual rainfall of 602 mm, beautiful parks and gardens, fine public buildings and lovely homes. An important distributive and industrial centre, it is the headquarters of Zimbabwe's railway system. The surrounding country is noted for its cattle ranching, and the mines in the area produce nearly half of Zimbabwe's mineral output.

62 Bulawayo's colourful Central and Centenary Park complex, with its myriad flowers, shrubs and trees and its miniature railway and model boating pond, is an irresistible recreational magnet for visitors and residents. Here, too, is the spectacular 75th Anniversary Fountain which at night hurls toward the stars its crystal cascades to a variety of heights, shot with a rainbow of colours.

63 The National Railways' Museum in Bulawayo houses a fascinating array of antique rolling stock and steam locomotives, including this Jack Tarr.

64 The Colosseum-style Natural History Museum is in Bulawayo's Central and Centenary Park complex. One of its many treasures is a huge fossilised egg laid over 2 000 years ago by the extinct *Aepyornis maximum* of Madagascar. The museum is the custodian of both the National Ornithological and Mammal Collections which took decades to compile.

65 A realistic construction at the Natural History Museum of a lion kill of a zebra. There are many other similiar animal displays, including the museum's famous mounting of the impressive Doddieburn Elephant which, standing 3,5 metres at the shoulder, is one of the largest mounted elephants known. The tusks alone weigh 40 kg and 41 kg.

62

66 Every April/May, Bulawayo plays host to the nation's International Trade Fair, symbolised here by the Fair Spire. This annual opportunity is taken by Zimbabwe and many other nations from Africa and other continents to put their finest products on display.

67 Like many Zimbabwean cities and towns, Bulawayo is built around a city square. Here, its City Hall is imposingly set in its own lovely gardens where there are colourful stands for curio and flower sellers; bead, basket and crochet workers; and artists.

63

66

64

65

67

The Legend of Nyaminyami

SEVENTY-FIVE million years ago, the Zambezi Valley nurtured embryo mankind. Less than four decades ago, it was still an unspoilt wilderness, the home of a small unsophisticated people called the BaTonga, and of a spectrum of wild animals and bird life.

But the might of the Zambezi River held too much promise for modern technology. As early as 1914, its flow was measured; shortly before World War II, a report was made on the possibility of building a hydro-electric scheme in the area. In 1950 a start was made. For the people of the Valley, it was a heartrending sight. Bulldozers roared instead of lion, smashing down centuries-old trees, hacking a road out of the savage terrain towards what would eventually become the dam wall.

Not only peace and solitude were taken away from the BaTonga; they were told to leave their homes because these would be flooded by the waters of the lake that would form. New settlements were built for them on higher ground, but before they moved, they swore that Nyaminyami, the River God,

69

would destroy the man-made abomination. For several years, it seemed that Nyaminyami was indeed venting his wrath. In 1958, near-disastrous floods wreaked havoc on the half-built dam wall. Over 16 million litres of water per second deluged the workings, washing away heavy equipment and almost all else.

By early 1959, the dam wall was completed, and the plains began to flood. Perhaps Nyaminyami was appeased by a new phenomenon: the advent of a cash economy for his people. The BaTonga began to fish for profit, and many now own flourishing sardine fleets.

There was no such consolation for the animals of Kariba. As the waters rose, their old haunts disappeared. Frantically, they tried to make for the remaining islands, hitherto deadly enemies swimming side by side, united in their last-ditch quest for survival. It was then that game ranger Rupert Fothergill and his team stepped in, with their flotilla of craft, encouraging the more hardy animals to swim to safety, capturing the weak and inept, tranquillising them for the journey, and finally releasing them on safe shores to find new homes. "Operation Noah", as it was dubbed, rescued over 5 000 animals, comprising 35 different mammal species let alone thousands of reptiles.

On May 16th, 1960, Britain's Queen Elizabeth flicked a switch to start the Kariba generators, and one of Africa's most ambitious projects officially came to life, bringing with it a vista that, once seen, few can forget. The dam wall rises 128 metres from the river bed. Behind it, Lake Kariba stretches back for 290 km, covers 6 000 sq km, is 42 km across at its widest, and has an average depth of 18 metres. The statistics, though, prepare one little for the sight of this inland sea which melts constantly from azure to aquamarine to amethyst and, at sunset, becomes a vast sheet of molten copper.

The sounds of Kariba are a study in contrasts: speedboat screams as holidaymakers at the excellent resort hotels waterski; a slower putter as amateur fishermen seek quiet inlets to hunt for Tiger Fish, bream, chesa, and giant vundu; the dawn murmur of a gulping shore, and the shriek of the Fish Eagle.

Operation Noah's animals were released on the shores of the Matusadona National Park, and obeyed the biblical injunction to go forth and multiply. Today, there are game viewing safaris by boat aplenty, but Bumi Hills, a resort 64 km south-east of the dam wall and set 121 metres above the water on a promontory, is a prime viewing point. Watch at sunset, and you may see elephant, buffalo, kudu and—if you're lucky—lion coming down to the water's edge to drink.

At the time of flooding, the tops of many trees remained above water. The mopane and leadwood trees (among the world's hardest woods) lost their foliage and died, but did not rot immediately. Without their leaves, and because of the hardiness of their wood, they appear to have fossilised. Today, these stark sentinels are the home for an increasingly rich bird population, winging its way from other parts of Africa and from Europe.

Kariba town is high on the heights overlooking the lake. Here stands St Barbara's open-sided church built in the shape of a coffer dam by the dam workers in memory of those colleagues who lost their lives during its construction. A big attraction, of course, is the crocodile farm. And then, what better than a voyage on the *Sea Lion*, a 22-hour ferry service with overnight facilities, which plies the length of the lake, bearing cargo, passengers and vehicles to various ports of call.

Apart from exploring Kariba, there are canoe safaris from the Kariba Gorge to Chirundu, and then the wonder of the Zambezi River. Covering over 250 000 ha, Mana Pools National Park lies astride the Middle Valley. With its camping sites, lodges and thatched cottages, Mana is, quite simply, enthralling. Elephant are its most spectacular extras in the crowd scenes here, although buffalo rival them—herds of up to 2 000 have been spotted. Impala, waterbuck and baboon also abound, and lion and leopard are not uncommon.

The Zambezi has always been the artery of Central/Southern Africa. Take time out to experience it and its lake child, and listen to the pulse of the mighty continent.

78

79

81

76 Standing bleached and stark against the blue Kariba skies, the tops of the mopane and leadwood trees are all that remain of the valley in which the lake formed. The trees died but did not rot immediately, and now appear to have fossilised.

77 Neither the old Cape buffalo grazing on the lake's water-logged grass nor the bream fisherman appears to be disturbed by the presence of the other. Although Kariba is renowned for its bream, to date 44 species of fish have been identified in the lake. There are active commercial fisheries for bream and kapenta (a small sardine).

78 A Fish Eagle takes off from its perch in a dead tree to hunt for bream.

79 Known in local lore as "The Lightning Bird", it swoops over the water when it sights a fish, talons outstretched.

80 Just before the surface, the Fish Eagle checks its incredible speed so precisely that only its talons enter the water to snatch the fish a couple of centimetres below the water. The Fish Eagle builds its nest of twigs in the branches of a large tree. Here the female lays two eggs, unperturbed by Kariba's sudden, fierce winds.

81 A Tiger Fish catch. This fish attains its greatest size in Kariba's waters with a record catch of over 15 kg. It is a doughty adversary for the angler, fighting, feinting and indulging in marvellous acrobatics to evade capture. Its razor-sharp, interlocking teeth can inflict a nasty wound. Moreover, anglers should beware because where there are Tiger Fish there are often crocodiles. Until recently, Tiger Fish was regarded as fit for sport only, but Zimbabwean restaurants now feature it in cocktail and smoked forms on their menus.

80

82

83

84

82   Caribbea Bay is one of several lakeside resorts offering every conceivable facility for relaxation and enjoyment. The water in its beach area and boat jetty is chemically treated to rid it of the Bilharzia parasite which is widespread in African waters.

83   Kariba boasts a casino offering blackjack, roulette and *chemin de fer* for those not too tired after a day on the lake or its shores.

84   The climate lends itself to outdoor activities and all the resort hotels provide one or more swimming pools in exotic settings, as here at Caribbea Bay.

85   Caribbea Bay has Sardinian-style casitas which echo the Mediterranean feel of Kariba.

86   Young crocodiles are lucky to be reared at Kariba's crocodile farm, but this one, resting in the branches of a submerged, dead tree in the lake, has to fend for himself. The reptiles do not interact, and at an early age must learn to survive alone, feeding off frogs, small fish and insects.

87   Potential rain clouds gather over the Matusadona mountain range viewed here from the headwaters of the Ume River.

88 Two waterbuck are frozen in silhouette against the burnished sky of a Kariba sunset. They are found in small herds, usually near water, are shy and, if frightened, have been known to bolt into the water to escape.

89 Spurwing Island, with Fothergill Island in the distance. Facing the Matusadona Mountains and Sanyati Gorge, Spurwing offers a unique experience in safari camp style. In addition to cabins and chalets, its luxury tents are erected under individual, cooling thatch to beat the heat. Game-viewing and fishing facilities, in the company of guides, are offered.

89

90

90 Fothergill Island has a safari camp with comfortable thatched chalets and, similarly, provides game-viewing, photographic and fishing excursions accompanied by expert guides.

91 The *Sea Lion,* loading here at Kariba's Andora Harbour, provides a 22-hour ferry service for cargo, passengers and their vehicles on the 290-km length of the lake to various ports of call. Meals and overnight accommodation are provided on board.

92 Waterbuck on the Kariba shoreline at Bumi. Because they have horns, which are long and curve outward and then forward, these are rams—young, about two years old. Note the distinctive white ring waterbuck have on their buttocks.

91

93 This lone hippopotamus is uncomfortably close. Its enormous size will topple all but the largest boat, and game-viewers normally give these mammals a wide berth. Hippo stand up to 1,5 metres at the shoulder, weigh up to 2 270 kg and, if disturbed, can be dangerous and aggressive, particularly during the mating season.

94 A tranquil scene of hippo resting toward the end of the day. Gregarious, they keep together in small communities, spending their days swimming or walking on the bottom of a river, coming out at night to feed on grass, water weeds and other vegetation.

95 It is unusual to see lion in water. At Mana Pools, this mature lioness has taken to the water either to reach an island in the Zambezi River in search of prey or is returning to the mainland to rejoin her pride. Lions feed on warthog (their favourite), zebra, buffalo and large antelope.

96 Alert, but not alarmed, this young black rhinoceros bull, at Matusadona National Park, inquisitively approaches the safari Land-Rover from which this photograph was taken. These animals have poor sight, but their sense of smell and hearing is acute. They are dangerous, and will charge with little provocation. In Zimbabwe, black rhino occur naturally and only around Lake Kariba and along the Zambezi Valley, although some have been translocated to Hwange National Park. It is a specially-protected animal.

93

94

95

96

49

97

98

99

100

97 Driven by age-old instinct, this herd of elephant follows, from a Kariba island, what was once an ancient game trail, before the lake waters rose, to reach Changachirere on the mainland in the Matusadona.

98 The presence of humans has clearly disturbed this large elephant bull, weighing up to five tonnes, whilst drinking on the shoreline. To show his irritation, an elephant sometimes makes a mock charge, fanning his ears and trumpeting angrily. However, it is never wise to take a chance that an elephant's charge is not real.

99 The Yellow-Billed Hornbill is often found waddling clumsily along the ground, and is slow in flight. It is found in mopane country, as here at Matusadona National Park.

100 Game viewing by boat on the mainland shoreline near Fothergill Island. Obviously aware that elephant can travel at speeds of up to 40 km/h for short distances, the helmsman keeps a hand on the throttle, even though the huge tusker does not appear to be unduly worried.

101 This is an interesting study of two mature elephant bulls. The one on the left is fanning his ears to keep cool, while the other is obviously left-handed as the tip of his left tusk is more worn than his right, indicating that he uses the left tusk more.

102

103

105

102, 103 & 104   A wildlife drama with a twist to the ending. This Wahlberg's Lizard had attacked the Side-Striped Sand Snake and appeared to be the victor once it had the snake's head in its mouth. But the snake managed to coil itself around the lizard, exerting pressure until the lizard weakened enough for the snake slowly to free its head from the lizard's mouth. The snake then struck at the lizard, immobilising it with its venom, and swallowed the lizard whole.

105   Another wildlife drama between two very much larger protagonists took place on the Bumi shoreline. A young, vagrant hippo bull tried to take over a herd of a dozen hippo cows and calves from the older, dominant bull. Accompanied by awesome roars, the fight raged for an incredible 14 hours. Although neither bull was killed, as so often happens in contests of this kind, each inflicted deep injuries on the other. The older hippo lost the territorial battle and slunk away to recover from his wounds. Thereafter, he will live as a loner or join a couple of other bachelor bulls. The younger victor will enjoy his spoils until challenged by another aspiring leader.

106   A unique way to experience the magic of Kariba is on a Water Wilderness Safari. Operated by Bumi Hills Safari Lodge, Water Wilderness provides water-borne accommodation in safari craft which offer every facility, including a private verandah on each craft. Part of the floating complex, which is based on the Chura River, a tributary of the Ume River, are (left) a mobile game-cruise craft, with a viewing platform atop, which doubles up as a diningroom and bar; (front right) a mother craft with kitchen, game guide's quarters; and (rear) a tree hide which affords unobtrusive and unsurpassed views of both water and land-based wildlife. The green carpet on the water is *Salvinia auriculata,* or Kariba Weed, which is found in sheltered bays, as here.

106

104

107 A mature leopard male with its kill at Mana Pools. Leopard are highly successful hunters because their dappled coats allow them to blend in with almost any terrain. Consequently, although they can run faster than most of their prey for short distances, they kill by ambush.

108 There can be few sights more breathtaking than an enormous herd of buffalo crossing from a Kariba island to the mainland or coming down to the shore to drink, as here. Herds vary in size from ten to well over a thousand, and are never very far from water.

109 A young lion male in the open grasslands in the Mana Pools area. He is either resting after a kill or is lying in ambush. The day is cool, otherwise he would opt for the shade of a tree or bush.

110 Warthogs love a wallow in the mud as this one was doing. They evoke laughter in human visitors because of their comical, stiff-legged trot and gallop and the way they hold their tails perfectly upright while doing so. Warthog is a game delicacy in camps and hotels and restaurants. They are also the favourite prey of lion, who dig them out of their holes. The Cattle Egret are commonly called Tick Birds because it is thought that they feed off the ticks on animals. This is not so. The birds eat the insects disturbed by the animals as they graze.

109

111 This old buffalo bull, past his prime, is part of a small bachelor herd of ten living on the Kariba shoreline. Buffalo have heavy, curved horns which meet at the forehead. This forms what is called the boss which protects the front of the head. They are dangerous when angered or wounded and have been known to savage their tormentors, human or animal.

108

110

111

The Mountain Paradise

THE Eastern Highlands encapsulate the diversity of Zimbabwe's visual riches. It is a story of mountain, valley, waterfall and stream. Yet, how the tempo changes as the sweep progresses 300 km, from austere Nyanga in the north, through the sensual allure of the Vumba to the lonely splendour of the Chimanimani in the south, thereafter the great primeval forests giving way to a pastoral patchwork.

Nyanga lies at the north end of a long mountain chain. Its plateau is at an altitude of 2 133 metres, rising to 2 592 metres at the summit of Mount Nyangani where the unwary are said to become invisible and disappear forever on its mist-shrouded slopes. As one approaches Nyanga, the mountain range appears gradually, rippling away in cerulean waves to lap at an equally blue horizon. Then the forests and myriad streams appear—but in early winter, the roads are incandescent with yellow wattle, a line of golden sunbursts against the sombre backdrop of pines.

Gracious hotels of international repute offer every comfort, from roaring log fires and traditional teas to the castanet song of the roulette wheel. The serious Nyanga devotee, though, will want to spend most hours roaming the enchanting Nyanga National Park and the surrounding areas.

113

Pungwe is Nyanga at its most majestic with the Pungwe Falls plunging 243 metres through a deep, densely-wooded gorge. Eight kilometres away at Honde View there is a panoramic vista of the vast valley linking the mountains. Here, the Mutarazi Falls, Zimbabwe's highest, stream like mercury over a vertical escarpment 762 metres into the Honde Valley below.

The Nyangombe Falls are different again: frivolous crystal chandeliers cascading over rocks exquisitely chiselled by the elements. Lovely Nyamziwa are perhaps less spectacular but have their own evocative appeal—a place indeed for secret thoughts.

Nyanga's dams, too, have different faces. Mare, queen of them all, is set amid gently rolling valleys and downs; Rhodes is pretty and prosaic, the fisherman's delight; Udu has a more untamed flavour. Little Connemara is an unexpected pool of blue, as if a piece of the sky had fallen upon the dark upland moors.

Mutare is Zimbabwe's fourth largest city, and charms all comers. Cradled by granite mountains, bedecked with flamboyants, it also has a large aloe and cycad collection in its park. Mutare's museum includes a transport gallery; horse-drawn carriages and steam locomotives are just two of the attractions.

Just outside the city, there's the National Trust area of Murahwa's Hill with its famous Gong Rock (so named because it is shaped like an old dinner gong and, when banged with a stick, resounds like one).

The road to the Vumba winds upwards from Mutare climbing 609 metres to the junction at Cloudlands. If Nyanga's air can be likened to dry champagne, then that of the Vumba is a cabernet: rich, heady, mellow. It is kind to vegetation; the Vumba Botanical Gardens are 30 ha of terraces crammed with flowers and shrubs. Although the spring garden in August is a joy, the end of the year is equally breathtaking when the pinks, blues and lilacs of hydrangeas, fuchsias and begonias are put on display.

Set in the Vumba Mountains, the Leopard Rock Hotel affords a spectacular view and is well worth a visit. Before it, far below, lies the tropical beauty of the Burma Valley; behind it is Chinyakwaramba, "the hill that sat down". Folk lore has it that the people who once lived here displeased the spirits, who caused the mountain to crumble and envelop them. Today, though, no bad vibes remain to disturb the tranquil loveliness of this spot.

The next call must be the Chimanimani Mountains. Fifty kilometres long, they rise to a height of 2 440 metres. There's a fairytale quality about them: the white quartzite sparkles in the sun like a sugar candy mountain, beckoning, promising. Mists veil the peaks in the early morning, but lift to reveal unparalleled beauty: crystalline streams are bordered with ferns and orchids, massed purple lassandria, bushes of wild sweet peas, traveller's joy and the sugar-pink Zimbabwe creeper with its fragile bell flower, tangle in profusion. Come winter, the ground is a treasure trove of protea. An ancient pathway leads up into the mountain fastness passing cedar and yellow-wood trees. Laughing doves, larks, eagles, swallows and swifts are the familiars of these forests. Watch out for eland: the Chimanimani has a protected herd of these, the largest of antelope. The region glitters with falling waters, and without doubt the most intrinsically beautiful of them all is Bridal Veil Falls with its delicate water tracery spilling 50 metres into a natural swimming pool.

At the far end of the Eastern Highlands you will encounter the Chirinda Forest—647 ha of immense trees, jade-vaulted. Lord of this forest is the Big Tree, a 600-year-old red mahogany, 66 metres high, with a trunk 15 metres in circumference. Time stands still here, as indeed it does in all the Eastern Highlands, with sunlight and shadow chasing each other silently in a game as old as the gods themselves.

114

115

112   An eagle's eye view of the fertile Honde Valley 800 metres below, as seen from the top of the Mutarazi Falls. Much of Zimbabwe's tea is grown on plantations in the Honde.

113   The green spaciousness of the Eastern Highlands is no more evident than here on the outskirts of Chimanimani town, looking toward the towering crags of the Chimanimani Mountains.

114   The Black-Headed Oriole is a common sight in the forests of the Eastern Highlands.

115   The Mountains of the Mist that are the Vumba Mountains provide a magnificent setting for the Leopard Rock Hotel. It has an elegant casino, and its international championship golf course, judged the best in southern Africa, is a spectacular spread of fairways and greens carved into a landscape of breathtaking grandeur.

116   The Vumba Botanical Gardens were created by a dedicated gardener, Mr Fred Taylor, who later bequeathed them to the nation. Two of its renowned attractions, fuchsias and ancient fern trees, are visible here, but in the background lie its wealth of indigenous trees.

117   Herbert Chitepo Street, Mutare, capital of Manicaland Province. The city is a bowlful of colour the year round: misted with jacaranda in spring, blazing with flamboyant blossoms at Christmas, and resplendent in the pink and yellow of aloes in winter.

118   The charming Nyachohwa Falls, tumbling into a natural woodland pool, always come as a delightful surprise to tourists. The Falls are situated on the Nyachohwa River 20 km from Mutare on the Burma Valley Road.

116

117

118

119   The unspoilt beauty of Nyanga's dams and rivers contribute much to its attraction. The gentle waters (as here at Little Connemara) enable the visitor to be at one with nature, inhaling the clean, fresh air and listening to the song of the wind in the pines.

120   Bushbuck are found in thickly-wooded country throughout Zimbabwe and are common in the Eastern Highlands. They are small, shy antelope frequently seen browsing on the edge of thick bush. The short, slightly cork-screwed horns of the ram easily distinguish it from the female, which is hornless.

121   As its name implies, the Paradise Flycatcher feeds on small insects and inhabits forests, preferably those with streams or rivers running through them.

122   The peace and tranquility of Nyanga National Park can be experienced by visitors in the comfortable one- and two-bedroomed cottages and lodges. All are fully furnished, equipped and serviced and are ideal for families and honeymooners.

123   Beautiful Mare Dam is situated in the uplands beyond the Montclair Hotel. Nearby lie the trout hatcheries, where many thousands of trout fingerlings are raised for eventual release into park waters and private streams. Here, also, secluded park chalets, fully furnished, equipped and serviced are available.

123

120

121

122

124

125

124 The Scarlet-Chested Sunbird, one of the most spectacular of the species, is commonly sighted singly or in pairs in Nyanga. It breeds here, in the Middle Zambezi Valley and on the central plateau, including Hwange and Matabeleland. Its long, slender, curved bill enables it to suck the nectar from tubular flowers.

125 Facilities for a host of sporting activities are available in Nyanga, but the golf course at Troutbeck Hotel is a special delight with its incomparable surroundings. The hotel's lake, part of it seen here, is stocked with trout for residents to fish and either take their catch home or have it prepared and cooked for them by the hotel.

126 Pony trekking in the early morning mist. All the Nyanga hotels provide pony trekking facilities—an invigorating way of exploring the unspoilt countryside.

127 The lovely Chapungu Falls, on the Scenic Drive which winds its way round Nyanga, are named in Shona after the Bateleur eagles which rule the skies in this area.

126

128

128   The Bird of Paradise *(Strelitzia)* is one of Zimbabwe's most exotic flowers. It is sometimes called the Crane Flower after the crest on the head of the Crowned Crane. So favoured is the flower by visitors to Zimbabwe that many take boxes of it home with them.

129   Nyanga is renowned for its trout fishing. Rainbow and Brown Trout are the most common in these waters, but American Brook Trout and the hybrid Tiger Trout are to be found also. The Rainbow average about 0,33 kg in the streams, and larger specimens can be caught in dams and lakes.

130   At 2 592 metres, Mount Nyangani is the highest point in Zimbabwe. Seen here just after the onset of the summer rains, the countryside is acquiring its carpet of soft new grass, providing an emerald contrast to the indigo heights.

131 A causeway across the Pungwe River in Nyanga National Park's natural countryside. The roof of one of the park lodges can be glimpsed through the green veil of the wattle and pine trees.

132 The Chimanimani Mountains contain a number of fairly easy trails for hiking. Some, further into the mountains, pose a real challenge to the more experienced climber.

131

133 No visitor to Nyanga should miss the breathtaking vista afforded by the spectacular Pungwe Gorge. The Pungwe River drops 240 metres into this thickly-wooded, ten kilometre-long gorge and continues into Mozambique, entering the Indian Ocean at Beira.

132

133

134

135

136

134 Situated on the western edge of the Nyanga Mountains, close to the gentle Connemara Lakes, World's View provides a vast, stunning vista of the plain and Nyanga North 600 metres below. On a clear day, one can see to the Mozambique border.

135 A particular attraction for visitors to Nyanga are the Nyangombe Falls where a myriad small cascades fuse for the headlong rush into the deep green valley below. The Falls are on the Nyangombe River, near Udu Dam where comfortable park chalets are a favourite weekend or longer retreat for holiday-makers.

136 One of the many pine forests grown commercially in Nyanga and Chimanimani. Although not indigenous to Zimbabwe, the pine has made itself very much at home in the country, particularly in great hills toward the eastern border. Both Government and private enterprise are actively involved in afforestation schemes.

137 Beautiful specimens of *Aloe arborescens* appear to have taken over Nyangwe Fort in eastern Nyanga, with the Nyangani Mountains forming a majestic backdrop. A vast complex of ruined forts, pits, enclosures, terraces and water furrows cover some 7 500 square kilometres of the Nyanga district. At Nyangwe Fort, a community (as yet unidentified) sheltered from invaders: there are crop terraces, the remains of dwelling places and so-called "slave pits" into which cattle were probably herded at night as protection from marauders, both human and animal.

138 A doorway into Nyangwe Fort shows the dry-wall construction of cut granite stones. A skeleton of Late Iron Age Man was found near here.

137

138

140

139 A popular picnic spot is at the Bridal Veil Falls, in Chimanimani, with its delicate water tracery spilling for 50 metres over rock steps to a natural swimming pool. The lush greenery is typical of this region, which combines the grandeur of Nyanga with the more tropical foliage of the Vumba.

140 Vervet monkeys are an intrinsic part of the Zimbabwean countryside and can be spotted frequently near built-up areas where they like raiding fruit trees. Inquisitive, clownish, they can become reasonably tame and apparently friendly but, when alarmed or annoyed, will bite. In the Eastern Highlands, their largest predator is the leopard.

141 The Nyanga and Chimanimani Mountains are leopard country. These splendid animals live a solitary existence and are seldom seen by day. The antelope, monkeys, baboons and small mammals which abound in the mountains provide it with a plentiful diet.

142 The Honde Escarpment drops a dizzying 800 metres from the Nyanga National Park to the Honde Valley below. Cloaked in a kaleidoscope of Africa's unique spring (October) colours, as shown here, the craggy face of the escarpment is host to three water falls. Just discernible in this picture are the Matururu Falls. However, the highest of the three, and indeed the highest in Zimbabwe, are the Mutarazi Falls which drop 762 metres in two stages down the sheer cliff. So rugged is the protecting rock of the escarpment that neither the Mutarazi nor the other falls has satisfactorily been photographed.

141

142

Kingdom of the Ancients

GATEWAY to the Lowveld is the Save River and Birchenough Bridge, a silver arch which, when it was opened in 1935, was the third largest single span bridge in the world.

Masvingo is the capital of Masvingo Province, heartland of the Rozvi dynasty which once ruled from the Gwayi River to the Indian Ocean. In the 19th century, Masvingo was the site of the first mud huts built by Cecil Rhodes' occupying forces. A turbulent history behind it, Masvingo, with its wide gracious streets, is the centre for a thriving agricultural, industrial and mining region. Its most renowned neighbouring attraction is the tiara that comprises Great Zimbabwe, Lake Mutirikwe and the Kyle Game Reserve; but in the very south-east lies Gonarezhou, The Place of the Elephants—137 000 ha of beautiful wilderness. During the Cretaceous Period, this was an inland sea dominated by giant reptiles and to this day waterworn rocks and littoral deposits characterise the plains. Now, majestic animals are the kings of Gonarezhou. At Chipinda Pools, hippo gambol in the shallows, while the towering Chilojho Cliffs, coral pink in the morning and evening sun, are another special part of this inimitable Eden.

Great Zimbabwe was once a citadel and a holy place. The kings and high priests have gone, but the aura lingers on, and few who visit it do not come away a little more silent and pensive than usual, touched with awe.

144

Your first sight of the ruins, 29 km from Masvingo, is of a mighty wall, curling like a python around the crest of a rocky hill. This is the Hill Complex, built on the edge of a sheer granite cliff. Below it lie the Great Enclosure, where it is thought lived the ruling king's wives, and the Valley Complex, where lesser dignitaries dwelt. The ruins have proved a treasure trove for archaeologists—relics and artefacts of visiting civilisations have been unearthed, such as pottery, soapstone carvings, gold, copper and ivory jewellery and ornaments, many of which are in the nearby site museum.

Great Zimbabwe is composed entirely of granite blocks cut to a specific size and fitted together ingeniously without aid of mortar. Close on a million were used. Some were cut into small pieces for decorative edgings or insets—the distinctive chevron pattern is the most common. It is believed that building began, on the Hill Complex, between 1100 and 1150 AD. Carbon dating has established that much of the rest of Great Zimbabwe was built during the 14th century, and it is estimated that, at the time, about 30 000 people were living in the area. The subsequent abandonment of Great Zimbabwe probably took place because, with that number of people, water, grazing and firewood became increasingly scanty, and severe drought and a plague of locusts exacerbated the already serious environmental problem. Internecine quarrels and attacks from outsiders on what had once been a strong and united kingdom ultimately spelt its doom. Creepers and long grass grew over Great Zimbabwe and it lay silently in the sunlight, unseen by the outside world until a hunter, Adam Render, stumbled upon the amazing sight in 1867.

From the Hill Complex, a dazzling splash of vivid blue on the horizon arrests the eye. This is Mutirikwe, Zimbabwe's second largest lake. It is the fruit of one man's dream; a story of perseverance against all odds.

In the 1930s, south-eastern Zimbabwe was a harsh, inhospitable land suitable, it was thought, only for ranching. But Thomas Murray MacDougall had other ideas. He had established a farm between two rivers and had been fired by the idea of growing sugar. To irrigate his fields, he needed a lot of water and so began boring a tunnel 472 metres through a granite hill. With the rains came floods; in the dry season, the water flow slowed to a trickle; but after seven long years, he got it right and began his crops with three lengths of sugar cane. Finally, over the next ten years, MacDougall proved that sugar was a moneyspinner for the nation.

The Lowveld saw large-scale expansion, with the burgeoning of the sugar industry, the establishing of vast citrus estates and then the invaluable winter wheat crop. A massive water storage scheme was needed and so, in 1961, Mutirikwe Dam was built and its lake spread to cover 90 sq km. Other dams followed, and now the Lowveld is an endless sea of green, wave upon wave of lush crops sprouting in exuberant abundance.

Mutirikwe has an exotic flavour, with all the grandeur and mystery of an African lake; indigo-shadowed mountains crouching over it, lion-hued grass sprawling at its feet. The shoreline plunges from granite cliffs to tree-dappled rocky beaches, and the lake's many islands are rich with bird life. The game reserve on the northern shore has 64 km of winding roads and the biggest variety of antelope in the country.

Humans take their sport on and around Mutirikwe too; there's every kind of boating, and the fishing, especially for Black Bass, is excellent. But to enjoy Mutirikwe at its best, take a late afternoon cruise up the lake, as the sun sets like a breaking egg yolk over the crags of the Beza and Nguni mountains, and a fresh breeze ruffles the silken surface of the water. There is an indefinable *ambiance* at this time; and you then understand why the mighty Rozvi kings made this place their own.

143 The lowering skies above Great Zimbabwe seem to give point to the mystery, romance and fascination that have surrounded the ancient ruin for over a hundred years. It has been a fruitful hunting ground for innumerable archaeologists and anthropologists, a variety of conflicting theories have been expounded, books written and invaluable artefacts and relics uncovered, and still the preoccupation with its origins continues. The truth of the matter is that, although Great Zimbabwe was discovered by the European world in the late 19th century, the inhabitants of the area had known of it for over 700 years, and radio-carbon dating and archaeological evidence suggest that it was built in the 13th century. This picture shows the Valley Complex and the Great Enclosure, as seen from the Hill Complex.

144 The unique Zimbabwe Bird is a symbol today of the nation's cultural heritage. It is also the country's national emblem and is represented on its flag, currency and Coat of Arms. With two exceptions, all the remaining examples of the Bird were found within the Hill Complex and all but one are on view at the site museum. They average 355 mm in height and are sculpted from grey-green soapstone. It is not known whether the symbolic meaning of the birds was religious, dynastic or totemic.

145 As a citadel and a holy place, the Hill Complex was impregnable with the commanding views it had over the valley from the massive, crenellated walls. It took decades to build and legend has it that the kings responsible for the early structures at Great Zimbabwe decreed that each visitor to their court should bring at least three granite stones as tribute. In this way, gradually the materials for building were amassed.

145

146

146 Thought to be part of the defenses, a labyrinth of stairways and passages links various sections of the Hill Complex. So well crafted were these that, like the steps shown here, they have withstood the ravages of centuries.

147 The site of the Hill Complex was carefully chosen for prestige and defense—it stands on the edge of a sheer cliff, 80 metres above the valley. Originally, access was only through two routes (the Ancient Ascent, imposing and used only by visiting dignitaries; and the Watergate Path, used by the women to fetch water), and intruders were faced with having to scale the granite precipice.

148 The Conical Tower in the Great Enclosure in the valley below the Hill Complex is a solid stone structure ten metres high, with a base diameter of five metres. Its significance has been lost in the mists of time, but one of the many theories suggests that it represents a giant grain bin to portray the obvious wealth and importance of the ruling king.

149 The massive outer wall that surrounds the Great Enclosure is eleven metres high, five metres thick in parts and has a circumference of 255 metres. The Great Enclosure itself contains 18 000 cubic metres of stonework, which makes it the largest single ancient stone structure in sub-Saharan Africa.

150 The chevron pattern runs along the top of the outer wall of the Great Enclosure and is believed to represent "The Snake of Fertility" which ensures a continuing line of descendants.

151 The Great Enclosure, 106 metres at its widest, was constructed at a later date than the Hill Complex to house (so it is conjectured) the ruling king's senior and minor wives. Excavations within the Great Enclosure have exposed a ritual altar and various items of a feminine nature, such as necklaces and beads.

152 Part of the Modern Ascent, a walled passage leads to the Hill Complex. This ascent was used by the women of the community on their daily ritual of fetching and carrying for the king and his senior court members. It was, in effect, a rear entrance to the Hill Complex so that the women did not use the main entrance, the Ancient Ascent. The monoliths protruding from the top of the Western Enclosure wall of the Hill Complex (background) are believed to be symbols of royalty.

153 The entrance passage into the Hill Complex leads from the imposing Ancient Ascent through the enormous Western Enclosure wall below the crenellations.

154 Outside the Great Enclosure, colourful aloes adorn the ruins of passages and dwellings where it is thought lived lesser dignitaries of the ruling king's court.

155 Inside the Great Enclosure looking up to the Hill Complex. An indication of the number of people who were housed in the Great Enclosure can be gauged by the extensive rock rubble remains of walls and passages.

156 Illustrating the sturdiness, the precision and the large scale on which most of Great Zimbabwe was built is this passage in the Great Enclosure leading to the Conical Tower.

152

153

154

155

157

157 A square-lipped (white) rhino cow and her calf rest during the heat of the day at Kyle Game Reserve. In marked contrast with the irascible hook-lipped (black) rhino, the white rhino is relatively genial and, here, does not appear to be disturbed by approaching humans. The game reserve covers over 8 000 ha and is home to a representative variety of wildlife—impala, zebra, giraffe, buffalo, blesbok, oribi, Lichtenstein's hartebeest. The adjacent recreational park provides chalets and caravan and camping sites on Lake Mutirikwe from which visitors can explore the game reserve and the picturesque countryside.

158 Close to Great Zimbabwe, lovely Lake Mutirikwe has the dusky blue Beza and Nguni mountains as a backdrop. Second only in size to Lake Kariba, Mutirikwe has a surface area of 9 165 ha and, when full, holds 1 332,6 million cubic metres of water. There's something for everyone at the lake. For the artist and dreamer, the scenic drive skirting the shoreline; sailing, water-skiing and powerboat racing for the watersport enthusiast; barbel, bottlenose, red-bellied bream and black bass aplenty for the fisherman.

159 Another beautiful Zimbabwean sunset, this time over Lake Mutirikwe and its dam wall. Built astride the Mutirikwe River in 1961, the concrete arch dam is 63 metres high and over 300 metres across.

160 The Secretary Bird is a member of the eagle family and is often seen striding importantly along open veld, either singly or in pairs. Contrary to the popular belief that it acquired its colloquial name from its prominent nape feathers, which look like the old quill pens, it is because of its black leggings, wing feathers and sober grey fronting, reminiscent of 19th century office clerks.

161 The glittering silver arc of Birchenough Bridge spans the Save River to connect the Eastern Highlands with the Lowveld. The Save's high flood waters and shifting sands precluded the use of piers, and so Sir Ralph Freeman, architect of the Sydney Harbour Bridge in Australia, designed this graceful single-span steel suspension bridge. When opened in 1935, it was the third largest such bridge in the world. It was named after a benefactor of the country, Sir Henry Birchenough, whose ashes and those of his wife are interred within one of the towers of the bridge.

162 A classic baboon posture. Part of a large troop, this adolescent has sought a high vantage point to keep a lookout for predators while the others forage below him. If danger is sighted, he will bark a sharp warning.

163 The soft, tangy fruit of the Monkey Orange Tree (*Strycknos spinosa*) is enclosed in a hard round shell which turns a yellow-brown when ripe, and only then is it edible. It is widespread in Zimbabwe and its ripe fruit is often stripped and eaten by baboons and monkeys.

162

163

164

165

166

164 In the Runde River, at Gonarezhou, this hippo bull is showing his irritation at the unwelcome presence of humans by gaping his mouth to display his huge canines (called tusks).

165 A characteristic of all mammals is their maternal caring. It is no less so with hippo, as in this touching scene of a yearling being shepherded by its mother, left, and a bull, possibly the herd sire.

166 It is unusual to see hippo and crocodile sharing a basking spot, as they are here at midday on the Runde River. Although the two species co-exist and leave each other alone, a large crocodile will snatch a young hippo calf—all predators are opportunists.

167 This verdant and tranquil scene on the Runde River shows the typical vegetation to be found on its banks. The Apple-ring acacia in the foreground is found only in the lowveld regions, as is the Fever acacia on the far bank. The Runde is one of the two largest rivers which drain the Lowveld. The other is the Save.

168 The Chilojho Cliffs are the most spectacular feature of the Runde River. Towering above the Runde Plain in the Gonarezhou National Park and Game Reserve, they are visible from 50 km away. Of special interest to geologists, the cliffs are composed of the most recent sediments of the Cretaceous Period, when most of the area was an inland sea believed to have been dominated by giant reptiles. No fossils have been found here, however.

169 Other striking features of the endlessly fascinating Runde River are the steep, rocky outcrops which flank her banks, as here in the mid-lower section in Gonarezhou.

170 Dwarfed by the impressive Chilojho Cliffs, a breeding herd of elephant ambles down to a pool in the Runde River to drink. Gonarezhou, meaning "Place of the Elephant", is the untamed heart of Zimbabwe and perhaps her most imposingly grand national park and game reserve. Apart from elephant, it has large concentrations of almost every species of wildlife—lion, giraffe, buffalo and a wide variety of antelope.

172

173

92

171 That these young elephant bulls were preoccupied with their playful wrestling is how this delightful close-up study came to be recorded in Gonarezhou. No longer the case, but because of the centuries-old history of hunting and poaching, elephant in this area are conditioned by herd behaviour still to keep a safe distance from humans.

172 In the Lowveld, buffalo occur mainly along the Save and Runde Rivers because they need plentiful grazing and water. These two bachelor bulls were part of a small herd found on the fringe of a riverine thicket in Gonarezhou.

173 A male baboon grooms a female in the troop by parting the fur and searching for and removing tiny flakes of skin. This behaviour is called "allogrooming" and serves to strengthen the bonds between individuals in a troop. Baboons live in troops of up to 200 which are controlled by six or seven dominant males such as this one.

174 The exquisite Sabi Star *(Adenium obesum)* blossoms forth from an unpromising-looking shrub which has a thick and distorted base, giving rise to its nickname of Baby Baobab. The flower has no scent. The stem provides a succulent treat for the larger antelope, such as kudu.

174

175 Gonarezhou can be hot and dry, and what better for a lion to do, when the sun is still high overhead, than to rest up in the cool, spreading branches of a fig tree. This tree-climbing behaviour is not common in southern African lion; it is normally associated with the Manyara lions in Tanzania.

175

VICTORIA FALLS AND HWANGE
A Savage Splendour

THE Zambezi River trickles to life in the highlands of north-west Zambia and meanders through the Barotse plains. Then the route becomes more hazardous, with rocky gorges to negotiate, some narrow, others over a kilometre long, and all of them now bearing testimony to the river's timeless travels. The last lap, taken at a gallop, passes through palm-fringed banks before the Zambezi becomes fretful and turbulent, gathering strength for its mighty leap over the cliffs to form what is now known to the world as the Victoria Falls.

"Scenes so lovely must have been gazed upon by angels in their flight." So exclaimed the first white man to set eyes on the mighty Falls, missionary-explorer Dr David Livingstone who happened upon their immensity and awesome grandeur in 1855 after approaching, intrigued, "five columns of vapour rising 250 feet to mingle with the clouds".

Five separate falls make up the Victoria Falls: Devil's Cataract, Main Falls, Horseshoe Falls, Rainbow Falls and Eastern Cataract. In flood season, 545 million litres of water a minute crash down the 100-metre height of the Falls along their width of 1 688 metres. Collectively, the Falls are twice as tall as those at Niagara and one and a half times as long. Nature has been generous in providing a magnificent viewing gallery. The Rain Forest, with its exotic lushness of ferns, lianas, orchids and "red hot pincushions", takes you right to the edge of the First Gorge and along its length—with umbrella and raincoat, if you are wise, for the drenching spray. Devil's Cataract comes first, with a 30-metre wide spread and 70-metre fall. When the Zambezi is at its height, the water races over its edge at speeds in excess of 160 km per hour. It is not hard to see how its name came about. There is something terrifyingly mesmeric about the white avalanche thundering down into the Stygian depths of the gorge—at this point a narrow, murky place of black rocks and furiously swirling waters.

The next falls you see from the Rain Forest are Main Falls where, over their 93-metre height and width of over a kilometre, cascades the Victoria Falls' major flow of water. Main Falls end at Livingstone Island where the explorer first stood in awe, breath catching in his throat at the spectacle before him. After Livingstone Island are the smaller Horseshoe Falls, narrow and crescent-shaped. Next come the tallest of the falls, Rainbow Falls. At 108 metres high, they are particularly enchanting with all the colours of heaven springing across the sky.

180

Finally, at the extremity of the Rain Forest's "grandstand" is the best of all vantage spots—Danger Point. From here you can view most of the 101-metre high Eastern Cataract and the Boiling Pot. Slippery and heart-in-the-mouth though Danger Point is, stand there with an ephemeral curtain of spray billowing and then shredding over your face and you experience almost the full grandeur and spirit of this mighty wonder of the world.

In addition to the memorable walk through the Rain Forest, you can also view the majesty of the Falls by light aircraft through the *Flight of Angels* service. Another experience is an afternoon or sundowner cruise up the Zambezi during which you will see crocodiles on the banks, cavorting hippos and, of course, the ubiquitous monkeys in almost every tree. Everything is larger than life at the Victoria Falls—witness the giant baobab tree, 16 metres in circumference, 20 metres high and up to 1 500 years old. The craft village shows you traditional Africa with all the structures of old village life. At night, the Victoria Falls Hotel mounts displays of traditional dancing, lit by flaming torches, and pulsing rhythms rise to the omnipresent stars. This is the message of the Victoria Falls: a magical place of natural, unspoilt wonder.

HWANGE National Park is one of the world's major wildlife reserves covering over 14 600 sq km. Its 107 species of animal and 401 species of bird can be seen from its four camps where cottages, lodges and chalets are available. Lovely Sinamatella Camp is 55 metres up on a plateau overlooking a vast plain. This is the favourite haunt of Hwange's elephant—some herds numbering several hundred apiece. Robins Camp is lion country, Main Camp is friendly and bustling, and Nantwich Camp is set in a remote spot overlooking a large, busy waterhole.

Hwange is animal magic and especially so from midday at the waterholes. At first an impala or three might appear, slender and jete-ing as any *corps de ballet*. Then perhaps a snuffling warthog, a few stalwart kudu or diminutive steenbok. After that, once the crowd gathers, there is almost too much for the eye. Zebra, mavericks in striped pyjamas; a giraffe, gentle and vulnerable, stilt legs spread as it stoops to drink, and then an elephant herd lumbers along ponderously. The prize, of course, is the lions arriving for their evening drink.

Night falls on Hwange like a black velvet shawl. Renewal begins only tomorrow, and you feel you are part of the purifying, pristine process.

181

182

179 An apricot dawn washes over a section of the world's largest and most magnificent waterfalls, the Victoria Falls. Here, after a journey of 1 200 km from its source in north-west Zambia, the mighty Zambezi River, the fourth largest river in Africa and the only major one to flow eastward to the Indian Ocean, reaches its awesome climax as it plunges down a vertical chasm. This spectacular picture, taken from Danger Point, is of part of the Eastern Cataract.

180 The massive rent in the earth, carved out by thousands of years of water turbulence, varies from 61 to 108 metres in depth. The force of the water—545 million litres per minute in the flood season—sends spray clouds spinning high into the sky, often reaching heights of over 500 metres. This gave rise to the ancient African name for the Victoria Falls of *Mosi oa Tunya,* The Smoke that Thunders. In the foreground of this view of the Falls complex is Devil's Cataract and, next to it on the far side, Cataract Island.

181 An almost complete panorama of the Victoria Falls in all their grandeur: Livingstone Island—named after the missionary-explorer Dr David Livingstone who, in 1855, from the island's grassy ledge, was the first white man to see the Falls; Horseshoe Falls—a small fissure being excavated in Livingstone Island by the river; Rainbow Falls—at 108 metres, the highest of the Falls; the Armchair—a natural rounded depression into which water rushes before spilling over into the gorge; Eastern Cataract—at 107 metres, the second highest of the falls. Missing from this view, on the left, are Devil's Cataract, Cataract Island and Main Falls. On the extreme right can be glimpsed Knife Edge Bridge, on the Zambian side of the Falls.

182 Echoing the curtain of spray that hovers and shimmers like gossamer in the sunlight, a rainbow arches perennially at the Falls. This picture shows the frenzy of the waters in the First Gorge caused by the millions of litres of water crashing down Devil's Cataract (out of sight on the left, toward the camera). On the left is Cataract Island, here obscuring half of Main Falls. On the right can be seen visitors at Main Falls Viewpoint in the Rain Forest.

183 The splendour of the Victoria Falls is a constant challenge both to the photographer and to the writer. Only by viewing them, as here at Eastern Cataract in full spate at the height of the flood season, hearing their thunderous roar, feeling their resonance transmitted through the rock on which one stands, and experiencing the gusty spray on one's cheeks, is it possible to absorb fully the majesty of this, one of the world's greatest natural wonders.

185

186

184 The rising sun underlining its primeval power, it is not difficult to understand how Devil's Cataract acquired its name. There is something terrifyingly mesmeric about the white avalanche thundering down into the depths of the First Gorge—at this point a narrow, murky place of black rocks and furiously savage waters. When the Zambezi is at its flood, the water races over the 30-metre width and 70-metre height of Devil's Cataract at speeds of over 160 km per hour. Here a flight of steps descends a third of the way down to the bottom of the gorge. Known as the Chain Walk, because of the chains to steady climbers on the slippery slopes, it culminates in a platform from which can be seen from below not only the final plunge of Devil's Cataract but a low level view of Main Falls.

185 No matter how often one gazes upon them, or from which vantage point, the Falls seem to acquire new dimensions, different personalities. Cooling in summer, threatening in winter, but always powerful, they provide a constantly changing spectacle. In this painting-like view of Eastern Cataract (from the pathway leading to Knife Edge Bridge in Zambia), the Falls reveal a regal bearing, framed by the ever colourful foliage its perpetual spray enriches.

186 Nature has provided a perfect grandstand in the Rain Forest—a spray-fed tropical jungle which runs parallel to the Falls along the top of the First Gorge for three quarters of the Falls' length. The network of paths lead at many points right to the lip of the gorge with head-on views, almost horrifyingly close to the roaring abyss. Visitors should take umbrellas or raincoats as the Rain Forest is continually drenched with spray.

187 After hurtling over the Falls, the water of the Zambezi frantically swirls in a feature known as the Boiling Pot where the First Gorge leads into the Second Gorge. In this view of the Second Gorge, from just beyond the Boiling Pot and under the Victoria Falls Bridge, can be seen the stately Victoria Falls Hotel at the top of the cliff, at the point where the Third Gorge develops.

188 Complementing Nature's master creation of the Victoria Falls is one of man's engineering feats: the Victoria Falls Bridge, spanning the Second Gorge just after the Boiling Pot. Completed in 1905, the railroad bridge was sited near enough to the Falls so that passengers on trains traversing it would feel the spray on their faces. The centre of the bridge marks the boundary between Zimbabwe and Zambia. From left to right are: the end of Main Falls, Livingstone Island, Horseshoe Falls, the Armchair and Eastern Cataract. The promontory at left centre is Danger Point which affords the most breathtaking of all the views of the Falls.

189 The Victoria Falls are in full flood in this photograph taken from above Cataract Island showing the complete width of Main Falls, ending at Livingstone Island. The volume of water thundering over the Falls is so great that an inpenetrable curtain of spray entirely cloaks the depths of the First Gorge. The bird's eye view into the chasm is from one of the light aircraft in the *Flight of Angels* service—a 20-minute aerial flip over the Falls.

190 The fury of the Zambezi River before its awesome leap. At his first glimpse of the Falls, David Livingstone entered in his diary for November 16th, 1855: "It has never been seen before by European eyes; but scenes so lovely must have been gazed upon by angels in their flight," and he named the Falls after his Queen, Victoria.

193

194

191 To give truly added dimension to the experience of the Victoria Falls, no visitor should miss the afternoon or sundowner cruise on the wide expanse of the Zambezi River on either the *Mosi oa Tunya* or the *Amanzi a Thunqayo*. The riverboats travel two kilometres upstream above the Falls to Kandahar Island and the Hippo Pool. Here, the rapid flow of water is suddenly impeded by a scattering of islands and, in the placid pools so formed, the bulbous grey hippos sport and snort. Crocodiles are often seen sunning themselves on the banks. Also in evidence are elephant, buffalo and other animals coming to the river to drink, and of course you can't miss the monkeys in almost every tree. David Livingstone was fascinated by the islands and planted coffee on one of them, convinced that the conditions there were ideal. Unfortunately, he had not bargained for the hippo, which fell upon the seedlings with delight.

192 In 1855, David Livingstone travelled downstream in a dug-out to the northern edge of the Falls precipice (at Livingstone Island) and first set his eyes on the wondrous sight. In a clearing near Devil's Cataract, facing the magnificent spread of the Falls, a memorial was erected to him. It records his birth on March 19th, 1813, at Blantyre, Scotland, and his death on May 1st, 1873, in what is now Zambia. His statue is cast in bronze and, today, he gazes serenely out for eternity over the scene which has since aroused in countless thousands of visitors the same incredulous awe he felt that November day so long ago.

193 Palm trees and the Zambezi are synonymous, and serve to heighten the strange, still beauty of sunsets across the river's now-placid waters.

194 The A'Zambezi River Lodge is an attractive, informal hotel complex which has the largest expanse of roof thatch in Africa. Strategically sited on the banks of the Zambezi upstream from the Falls, it enjoys commanding views of the mighty river and of the game which comes to its banks to drink. Accommodation at Victoria Falls is varied, with a choice of excellent hotels and serviced chalets in the town, fully-equipped cottages in the national park, camping in a centrally-situated restcamp and caravanning on the banks of the Zambezi.

195 The huge and tortuous baobab *(Adansonia digitata)* is a familiar sight in the Falls area, as indeed it is in all Zimbabwe's lowveld regions. It grows to an enormous size: one hollow baobab at Devuli River bridge is large enough to shelter 40 people within. Also known as the upside-down tree and the cream-of-tartar tree, folklore has it that at one time the baobab was the tallest tree in the world and, being so close to the heavens, was constantly giving advice to the gods. One day, in utter exasperation at its impudence, the gods uprooted the tree and replanted it upside down.

196 The Rainbow Hotel at the Victoria Falls has a Moorish design for maximum coolness. Continuing the cooling theme, the hotel sports a cocktail bar built into the swimming pool, accessible only to swimmers.

197 & 199 An *Africa Spectacular* is performed daily at the Victoria Falls Hotel. Some of the colourful and energetic performances in authentic costumes are a Shangaan war dance (197) and "The Hyena and Goat Dance" (199).

198 A craft village in Victoria Falls town depicts traditional rural life and arts, and includes a resident *n'anga* (witchdoctor) who can be prevailed upon to throw the bones and forecast the future for visitors.

200 The gracious Victoria Falls Hotel complements the majesty of the Falls. Built in 1915, the hotel has left many thousands of visitors with fond memories of its old-world elegance and service. From the comfort of its spacious verandah, the Falls bridge is clearly visible.

198

201

201　Fascinated tourists watch from an elevated walkway as these 1,2 metre crocodiles snatch and fight for meat during a feeding frenzy. The Victoria Falls crocodile farm, one of the finest in the country, provides guided tours daily. All aspects of crocodile biology are explained in layman's terms—from eggs and hatchlings (you may hold one, but be careful) to yearlings and two- and three-year-olds.

202　Enjoying a snooze in the sun, these crocodiles have recently fed, hence the very round individual in the centre who obviously eats a lot more than the others. Sunbathing is important for the health of these reptiles, and aids the digestion. An adult can grow up to a frightening 4,8 metres in length.

203　This view into a crocodile's gullet shows the throat valve (flaps of muscle) which closes off when the animal is submerged, enabling it to catch fish without swallowing water and drowning.

204　It's safe to hold a juvenile crocodile once you know how. The gape extends almost to the back line of the jaw, and the ear slit is situated just behind the eye which, here, is almost closed. The raised button on the upper end of the snout denotes the nostrils which, with the eyes, are all that appear above the surface of the water when the reptile is cruising around.

205　Gnarled as an old log, a crocodile heaves itself out of the water. Those bony and well-toothed jaws are used to catch fish and game. Teeth are replaced as soon as they break or fall out, the new ones erupting from underneath the old. This may occur several times in a crocodile's life, as it has more than two sets of teeth, unlike a mammal. Crocodiles are found in many rivers and pools and travel great distances overland at night. They are very dangerous and are responsible for more human deaths than any other wild species.

202

203

204

205

206 A magnificent study of a wind-swept, blond-maned king. Resting on massive paws, he looks regally disdainful as the grass, scorched to a golden brown, sways over him in a gusty dance of homage. Male lions form the focal point of stability in a pride's territory. If the pride's only mature male is killed, and there is no successor, the pride loses its integrity as a stable unit, and cub mortality rises. Once a new male is established in the pride, stability and protection are restored to it. Lion are widespread in Hwange National Park, with sightings regularly reported near Main Camp.

207 The yawn says it all; it's a long, hot day with nothing much going on. This young lion is in the peak of health, as is evident from his excellent upper and lower canines— vital to a lion, since with them he holds down and kills his prey.

208 "Getting twitchy" may well be used to describe this lioness, as the tip of her tail (front, right) begins to flick up and down in a clear sign of irritation. Lion are more frequently heard than seen, as their loud roars are well-known for carrying far on a still night.

209 Taking advantage of the cover afforded by a fallen thorn tree, a pride of four lionesses and an immature male (right, full face) blends well with the dry grass litter layer. Their easy, relaxed attitude belies the speed and strength with which they will react to sudden danger or to the sight of a potential meal.

210 Hwange National Park has the greatest concentration of elephant in Zimbabwe and, indeed, one of the greatest in the world. Breeding herds, such as this one, are normally led by the oldest cow, known as the matriarch. The herd is drinking at one of the many artificial waterholes created in the park because, apart from the four-month rainy season, there is no natural surface water. The trunks of some of the elephants are raised, sniffing the air, as the presence of humans is detected; but no alarm is evident.

211 Lacking confidence at this early age, a young elephant bull demonstrates anger by trumpeting, shaking his ears and running forward a few steps before stopping and kicking up dust. The loosely hanging trunk indicates that his charge is none too serious—the real thing comes with outspread ears and a tightly rolled trunk.

212 A particularly thirsty herd of elephant at one of the waterhole oases. Each sucks up a trunkful (about 15 litres) and squirts the water into the back of the gullet. Elephant normally drink first and then indulge in a mudbath (which they love) because their innate sense tells them not to foul their drinking water.

211

210

212

213

213 Taken from a hide, this close-up of a buffalo bull and two half-yearlings clearly shows the breadth of the bull's boss and the slightly undulating tips of his horns. The calves' horns will take at least five years to reach a similar size and shape. Herds of up to 2 000 buffalo are frequently sighted at Hwange. A number of hides have been constructed in the park to enable visitors to observe wildlife at close quarters in natural surroundings.

214 One of the largest flying birds, the Ground Hornbill is often seen at Hwange and in other lowveld areas. It occurs in small family groups which spend the day foraging through scrub for lizards, tortoises, locusts and other large insects. Its deep, booming call is normally heard at sunrise.

215 The superb contrast of white facial and belly markings with dark, sleek coats, topped by graceful scimitar horns, makes sable the most handsome of the antelope. Here, a bull (black coat, second from left) joins a herd of six cows at a tranquil waterhole. Although preyed upon by lion, sable are fleet-footed and more than capable of defending themselves, with scythe-like sweeps of their lethal horns. In fact, sable have been known to kill lion.

214

215

216

216 A Lappet-Faced Vulture (left, background) scraps with White-Backed Vultures over the remains of a lion kill. The vulture in the foreground is spreading its wings in a threat display against the others. A participant in the mêlée is a Marabou Stork—another scavenger.

217 Impala are renowned for their prodigious, graceful leaps when startled. Able to both graze and browse, depending on the season, they are found in a variety of habitats. The female herd here is under the control of the ram (foreground, with horns) whose territory obviously includes this section of a waterhole.

218 Southern giraffe are the only species of giraffe found south of the Zambezi River. Although spotted infrequently in various parts of Zimbabwe, giraffe are concentrated mainly in Hwange National Park and in the south-western Lowveld. They occur in small family groups of up to 25.

217

219 An open area of flooded grassland in Hwange National Park is the stage for this small herd of giraffe. The bull (extreme right) is larger and darker than the cows he is escorting. The two outgrowths on a giraffe's head are not horns but bony projections from the skull and are used by bulls when fighting each other during territorial (mating) disputes.

220 Perhaps at its most vulnerable, a giraffe needs to bend awkwardly at the shoulder and knee to reach water. A unique system of valves in the veins prevents blood pressure from causing blackouts when the animal lowers its head to hoof level. When attacked or frightened, giraffe will kick with their large feet, which are powerful enough to kill a lion.

221 Although they have similar (but shorter) horns, roan antelope are distinguished from sable by their black masks and white-ringed muzzles, long black-tufted donkey ears and grey-brown pelage. Slightly larger than sable, roan are less frequently seen. They generally occur in small herds of three or four, but some of 15-20 are sighted occasionally.

220

219

221

222

222 Pausing beside an anthill and a dead tree, a kudu bull listens and samples the wind with flared nostrils. The proud spiral of his horns reaches up toward the sky—one of them pale-tipped with maturity. The wither stripes of his coat break his outline and thereby help to camouflage his large body. Similarly, the white stripe between his eyes and on his upper lip break the outline of his head.

223 Ears outspread, necks stretched and muscles taut, two kudu bulls pause while drinking, having sensed danger. They will then leave the water with their characteristic high-stepping stride. Kudu are browsers and are often seen in the Main Camp area at Hwange National Park. Their ability to survive in harsh environments, despite continued hunting pressure, is an indication of their keen senses and speed.

223

224

225

226

227

224 Fully furnished and equipped lodges such as these are available at Main Camp in Hwange National Park. This camp is the central administrative headquarters for the whole of the park, which covers 1,3 million ha and contains more than 400 km of game-viewing roads.

225 Seen in most game parks in Zimbabwe, wildebeest (or brindled gnu) occur in herds of about 20. Essentially open plain animals, they rely upon their remarkable turn of speed to escape predators—normally lion, but also wild dog and spotted hyena. The young wildebeest (left), with their reddish-brown foreheads and short, straight horns, are distinguishable from the adults, whose horns curve up and inward above their black foreheads.

226 This untidy heap of seven young elephant, coated with black mud, happily avail themselves of Hwange Safari Lodge's hospitality. The waterhole is situated in front of the Lodge so that guests may enjoy an unobstructed view of all the game that comes to drink. Several "bunker" hides have been erected in the vicinity enabling game-watchers to get really close to elephant and other animals in safety at a range of half a metre or so.

227 Time for humans to refuel themselves. The daily buffet luncheon at Hwange Safari Lodge is an *al fresco* affair, in the cooling shade of huge indigenous trees.

228

228 Resplendent in red plumage, turquoise cape and with a long spectacular tail, the Carmine Bee-Eater is a familiar sight in Hwange from September to March. This bird is an intra-Africa migrant and breeds in huge colonies of up to a thousand in the sandy banks of some of the major river systems.

229 One of the smallest antelope, steenbok are frequently seen feeding at the side of the road between Main Camp and Shumba Pan in Hwange National Park, their dainty, diminutive forms blending perfectly with the dry grass. Like many other antelope, the ram has horns, while the female is hornless. They occur singly and pair off during the breeding season. The single lambs are born during the rains, from November to February.

230 The cool, comfortable thatched chalets at Robins Camp in the national park provide welcome respite for visitors, especially at the height of summer. There are three other well-equipped camps in the park—Main, Sinamatella and Nantwich. Visitors may go game-viewing in their own cars from all four camps, but need to return to camp before sundown for safety reasons. The variety of birdlife attracted to the camps is a particular delight. Some of the species to be seen are the Crimson-Breasted Shrike, Pied Babbler, Pygmy Goose and Crowned Crane.

231 This rare close-up of a cheetah clearly shows the spots on its coat and the dark tear line on either side of its muzzle. Normally an inhabitant of open plains dotted with anthills, this animal was moving through the scrub line at Hwange, possibly hunting steenbok or hares. The ruff on its neck and shoulders is raised, which means it is angry or frightened. The fastest animal over short distances, the cheetah has a smaller head and longer legs than the leopard, and is usually seen singly or in twos and threes.

229

230

232

232 The soft dawn light adds poetic shade to this tableau of a buffalo herd drinking at a rainwater-filled gulley. A peaceful scene such as this would be exploited by a watchful predator, ready to take any lazy stragglers or the weak and night-chilled. This is a small herd of about 200. Hwange has the greatest population of buffalo in Zimbabwe, and herds of up to 1 500 are not uncommon.

233 A snort of alarm and every animal gallops off in headlong flight, each for itself—male, female and young. Spooked, zebra and impala thunder through the Hwange woodland in herd panic at the threat of danger, whether real or suspected.

234 Photogenic in any situation, these zebra create symmetrical harmony in stripes as they slake their thirst at a well-used waterhole. Normally in small groups of a stallion and his five or six mares, they often band together to form large herds of 30 or more. Zebra establish a stable home range and seldom move from it except under drought stress.

234

233

235

237

236

235   Sensing danger, these alert Cape buffalo have formed a formidable phalanx of defence. Their keen sight and sense of smell enable them to identify quickly the source of their alarm. If it proves to be unfounded, they will resume grazing. Should the danger prove to be real, they will either take off in great lumbering strides or gang up on the predator and flush it from cover. The Red-Billed Oxpeckers in attendance are also known as tickbirds because they feed on the ticks which infest large animals. The birds act as alarms for the animals by emitting hissing sounds as they fly away at the first sign of danger.

236   The large, stately Saddlebill is a member of the stork family and the most colourful, with its red and black bill topped by a bright yellow saddle. Widespread in Zimbabwe, the Saddlebill breeds in Hwange National Park, where it is commonly sighted feeding at the edge of pans.

237   An elephant fight, for whatever reason, is not unusual. Possibly over the common issue of mating supremacy, these two bulls, tense and wary, squared off in mutual anger, ears flared, before clashing head-on and heaving against each other in a mute trial of colossus strength. In this instance, the only sounds were those of their rough skins rasping harshly together, punctuated by the clack of ivory against ivory. The battle ended almost as soon as it started, with no apparent victor, as they ambled off in separate directions.

238   The evening haze mingles with the dust kicked up by the frantic haste of the elephant herd in the background as it approaches a long-sought waterhole during a drought. Their thirst quenched, the five youngsters in the foreground, from an earlier herd, frolic in relieved tension.

239   The sweep and grandeur of the Eastern Highlands are a fitting epilogue for this portrayal of Zimbabwe. Of the many memorable scenes that have gone before, this view of the Pungwe Falls in Zimbabwe's mountain paradise best captures the essence of the splendour, the beauty and the freshness of a country still unspoilt and with so much to offer.

PHOTOGRAPHIC
CREDITS